Pete the

AND THE
COOL
CATERPILLAR

by James Dean

HOORAY!

_____

can read this book!

USA $3.99 / $4.99 CAN
ISBN 978-0-06-267521-7

harpercollinschildrens.com

S

Dear Parent:
Your child's love of reading starts here!

Every child learns to read in a different way and at his or her own speed. Some go back and forth between reading levels and read favorite books again and again. Others read through each level in order. You can help your young reader improve and become more confident by encouraging his or her own interests and abilities. From books your child reads with you to the first books he or she reads alone, there are I Can Read Books for every stage of reading:

SHARED READING
Basic language, word repetition, and whimsical illustrations, ideal for sharing with your emergent reader

BEGINNING READING
Short sentences, familiar words, and simple concepts for children eager to read on their own

READING WITH HELP
Engaging stories, longer sentences, and language play for developing readers

READING ALONE
Complex plots, challenging vocabulary, and high-interest topics for the independent reader

ADVANCED READING
Short paragraphs, chapters, and exciting themes for the perfect bridge to chapter books

I Can Read Books have introduced children to the joy of reading since 1957. Featuring award-winning authors and illustrators and a fabulous cast of beloved characters, I Can Read Books set the standard for beginning readers.

A lifetime of discovery begins with the magical words **"I Can Read!"**

Visit www.icanread.com for information
on enriching your child's reading experience.

www.icanread.com

Library of Congress Control Number: 2017943580
ISBN 978-0-06-267522-4 (trade bdg.) —ISBN 978-0-06-267521-7 (pbk.)

17 18 19 20 21 LSCC 10 9 8 7 6 5 4 3 2 1   ❖   First Edition

I Can Read!

BEGINNING 1 READING

Pete the Cat

AND THE COOL CATERPILLAR

by James Dean

HARPER

An Imprint of HarperCollinsPublishers

Pete is on a bug safari!

He and his friends
are looking for bugs.
How many bugs can they find?

5

Callie spots a tiny black ant.

"It's building an anthill!" she says.

"Groovy!" says Pete.

Gus finds a round red ladybug in
the mint patch.

"It has nine spots!" says Gus.

"Nice!" says Pete.

Marty sees a big black spider.

"It caught a fly," he says.

"Neat," says Pete.

Pete finds a green caterpillar
in the flowerpot.
"I will bring it home to show
Mom and Dad," he says.

Mom helps Pete build a home for

the caterpillar.

They use a big jar.

Dad puts lots of little holes in
the lid for air.

Pete puts the caterpillar
in the jar.

Pete puts some leaves in the jar
for the caterpillar to eat.

He adds a twig for it to crawl on.

"Good night, Pete," says Mom.

"Good night, Pete," says Dad.

"Good night, caterpillar,"
says Pete.

13

When Pete wakes up,
the caterpillar is gone!
Where did it go?
Did it run away?

"It is not gone," says Mom.

"It did not run away," says Dad.

"Look!" they say.

"The caterpillar is inside there,"
says Mom.

"It's called a pupa."

"Will it stay in there forever?"
Pete asks.

"No," says Dad. "The caterpillar is
changing into something new."

"What will it become?" Pete asks.

"It's a surprise," says Mom.

"We must wait and see."

Pete waits.

Callie comes to visit.

"Did it come out yet?" she asks.

"Not yet," says Pete.

Pete waits some more.

Gus comes to visit.

"Did it come out yet?" he asks.

"Not yet," says Pete.

Pete waits even longer.

Marty comes to visit.

"Did it come out yet?" he asks.

"Not yet," says Pete.

Pete waits

and waits

and waits.

22

Then, one day,

something finally happens.

The pupa starts to wiggle!

"Something is happening!" says Pete.

It wiggles some more.

Everyone comes over to watch.

The pupa cracks open.

Something is coming out!

What can it be?

A head pokes out,

then some legs,

and then two colorful wings.

The caterpillar changed into
a beautiful butterfly!
"Wow!" says Pete.

The butterfly slowly moves
its wings up and down.
It is ready to fly.

They take the jar to the park.

"Time to say goodbye," says Dad.

Pete opens the lid of the jar.

The butterfly flaps its wings.
It flutters out of the jar and
lands on Pete's nose.
"That tickles!" he says.

Then the butterfly flies up into

the sky.

"Bye-bye, butterfly!" everyone says.

"Let's find a new caterpillar!"

says Pete.

"Change is pretty cool!"